Dedicated to Aunt Bea

This is a book about BEES...

And their importance to me and you!

Since bees have survived for a very long time...

After 30,000 years -
They must know
what to do!

Being a popular insect - as bees were in Ancient Egyptian times...

Bees made their existence worth more than money…

Because something they made could be used in foods and medicines...

You guessed it right, if you said:
HONEY.

Honey can last a very long time...

In fact some honey was discovered in a tomb in 1922...

Scientists said it was over 3,000 years old...

I wouldn't try it....
What about you?

Honey begins life as flower nectar...

Inside the honeycomb it feeds the bees...

And now it's time to JUMP JUMP JUMP...

AND BUZZ LIKE A BEE!

Bees are natural helpers...

They move from flower to flower carrying and collecting nectar...

Flowers need bees and bees need flowers...

That's why bees have special powers!

Bees enjoy communicating with each other...

They have a very social way to meet!

No, they don't just ask...

Instead they waggle to the beat!

When bees transfer pollen grains...they help make our fruits and vegetables taste better.

Bees helping the planet isn't anything new.

And now it's time for you and me...

To JUMP JUMP JUMP

AND BUZZ LIKE A BEE!

Bees can fly up to 12 miles per hour...

That's 5.36 metres per second...

A bee vs. a squirrel would be a close race...

I think the bee would win, but what do you reckon?

Male bees called drones don't have stingers...

Female bees called workers do...

Bees have 5 hairy eyes but the colour red they can't see...

By flapping their two pairs of wings...

They create a BUZZING BEE FREQUENCY!

So come on let's JUMP JUMP JUMP AND BUZZ LIKE A BEE!

WE

BUZZY BEES!

Jump Series:
Jump Like a Caribou!
Jump Like a Kangaroo!
Jump at the Zoo!
Jump and Say P.U.!
Jump and Say Boo!
Jump and Say Valentine's Day Is
For Kids Too!
Jump and Look For a Clue!
Jump and Say Happy Birthday to You!
Jump For Everything Blue!
Jump, Hop and Say Happy Easter To
You!
Jump and Say Cock-A-Doodle-Do!
Jump and Sing Da-Do-Do-Do!
Jump and Ask Who? Who?
Jump and Squawk Like a Cockatoo!
Jump and Ask Is It You or Ewe?
Jump and Say There's an Ewww in My
Stew!
Jump and Say Merry Christmas To You!
Jump and Cheer Happy New Year!
Jump and Say There's a Moo-Moo in a
Tutu!

Jump and Say There's a Hare in My Hair!
Jump and Say My Aunt Ate An Ant!
Jump and Say There's An Aardvark In The Amusement Park!

Clap For Series
Clap for 1!
Clap for 2!
Clap for 3!
Clap for 4!
Clap for 5!
Clap for 6!
Clap for 7!
Clap for 8!
Clap for 9!
Clap for 10!

The Cat Who Said Hello
The Three Boulders
Billy Shakespeare
Billie Shakespeare
Learn To Draw With Symmetry
ABC More Learn to Draw With Symmetry

Non-Fiction
103 Fundraising Ideas For Parent
Volunteers With Schools and Teams